WITHDRAWN

MIAMI DOLPHINS

BRENDAN FLYNN

Apex is distributed by North Star Editions:
sales@northstareditions.com | 888-417-0195

Produced for Apex by Red Line Editorial.

Photographs ©: Tom DiPace/AP Images, cover, 1; Brennan Asplen/Miami Dolphins/AP Images, 4–5, 58–59; Rebecca Blackwell/AP Images, 6–7; AP Images, 8–9, 37, 57; Vernon Biever/AP Images, 10–11; Focus on Sport/Getty Images Sport/Getty Images, 12–13, 14–15, 22–23, 24–25, 38–39, 47, 50–51; George Gojkovich/Getty Images Sport/Getty Images, 16–17, 40–41; Kevin Reece/Getty Images Sport/Getty Images, 19; James Flores/Getty Images Sport/Getty Images, 20–21; Nate Fine/Getty Images Sport/Getty Images, 26–27; Rob Brown/Getty Images Sport/Getty Images, 28–29; Ronald C. Modra/Getty Images Sport/Getty Images, 30–31; Joel Auerbach/Getty Images Sport/Getty Images, 32–33; Megan Briggs/Getty Images Sport/Getty Images, 34–35; Stephen Dunn/Getty Images Sport/Getty Images, 42–43; Shutterstock Images, 44–45, 48–49, 54–55; Michael Reaves/Getty Images Sport/Getty Images, 52–53

Library of Congress Control Number: 2023924687

ISBN
979-8-89250-088-3 (hardcover)
979-8-89250-105-7 (paperback)
979-8-89250-138-5 (ebook pdf)
979-8-89250-122-4 (hosted ebook)

Printed in the United States of America
Mankato, MN
082024

NOTE TO PARENTS AND EDUCATORS

Apex books are designed to build literacy skills in striving readers. Exciting, high-interest content attracts and holds readers' attention. The text is carefully leveled to allow students to achieve success quickly.

TABLE OF CONTENTS

CHAPTER 1

FINS UP!

Tua Tagovailoa takes the snap. The Miami Dolphins quarterback looks downfield for a receiver. Suddenly, he's under pressure. A defender chases him toward the sideline. Finally, Tagovailoa sees what he was looking for.

Tua Tagovailoa threw for 309 yards and four touchdowns in a 2023 game against the Denver Broncos.

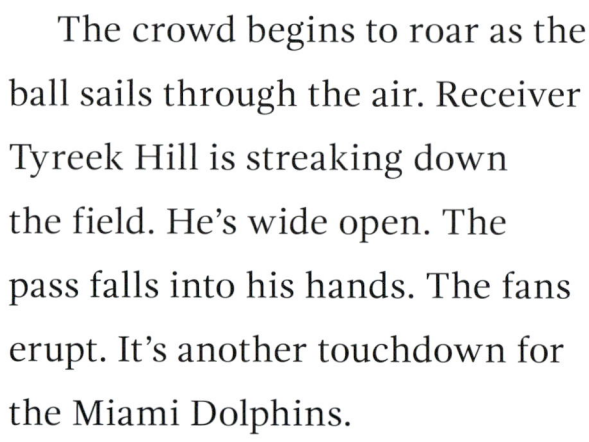

The crowd begins to roar as the ball sails through the air. Receiver Tyreek Hill is streaking down the field. He's wide open. The pass falls into his hands. The fans erupt. It's another touchdown for the Miami Dolphins.

WHY FINS UP?

The fin on the back of a dolphin makes it easy to recognize. So, when Dolphins fans feel like celebrating, some put their hands on their foreheads. Then they point their hands out like dolphin fins.

On September 24, 2023, the Dolphins beat the Broncos 70–20. It was the most points Miami had ever scored in a single game.

CHAPTER 2

EARLY HISTORY

The Miami Dolphins began play in 1966. They joined the AFL. This league was a rival to the NFL. The Dolphins were the AFL's first expansion team.

Running back Jim Kiick made back-to-back Pro Bowls in 1968 and 1969.

The Dolphins went 10–3–1 during the 1971 season. But they lost in the Super Bowl.

The Dolphins didn't win much at first. Then the AFL and NFL joined together in 1970. The Dolphins had their first winning season that year. They also reached the playoffs for the first time. The next season, Miami made it all the way to the Super Bowl.

ONE AND DONE

The Dolphins weren't the first pro football team to call Miami home. That honor went to the Miami Seahawks. They were formed in 1946. They played just one season before they folded.

In 1972, the Dolphins made history. They went 14–0 in the regular season. Then they won two playoff games. Finally, they beat Washington in the Super Bowl. The 1972 Dolphins became the first team to win the Super Bowl with a perfect record.

FAME AND FORTUNE

Danny Thomas helped found the Dolphins. He was also an entertainer. Thomas's fame stretched from the 1940s through the 1970s. He starred in many TV and radio shows.

Larry Csonka ran for 112 yards in the Super Bowl to cap Miami's perfect season.

Miami's defense dominated in the Super Bowl against the Minnesota Vikings.

The Dolphins' winning streak was snapped in Week 2 of the 1973 season. But they won their next 10 games. Then they rolled through the playoffs. The Dolphins repeated as Super Bowl champions. They beat the Minnesota Vikings 24–7.

NO-NAME DEFENSE

In the 1970s, several teams had defenses with catchy nicknames. But Miami's defense didn't have a lot of star players. An opposing coach said the Dolphins' defense had "a bunch of no-name guys." So, people started calling them the No-Name Defense.

The Dolphins had the look of a dynasty. But 1973 turned out to be their peak. They lost their first playoff game in 1974. Then they lost many stars. Some retired. Others moved on to different teams.

Miami made a surprise run to the Super Bowl in 1982. But Washington got revenge for its loss 10 years earlier. The Dolphins lost 27–17.

Running back Andra Franklin (37) made the
Pro Bowl in the 1982 season.

DON SHULA

Don Shula played defensive back in the 1950s. Then he turned to coaching. In 1970, he became the Dolphins' head coach. Shula quickly led Miami to two Super Bowl wins.

Shula fit his coaching to the strengths of his team. In the 1970s, the Dolphins had strong rushers. So, Shula built his offense around the ground game. In the 1980s, Miami drafted quarterback Dan Marino. Shula changed the offense. He began focusing on passing.

Shula coached the Baltimore Colts for seven years and the Dolphins for 26. He finished his career with 328 wins. As of 2024, that remained an NFL record.

DON SHULA WAS NAMED TO THE PRO FOOTBALL HALL OF FAME IN 1997.

CHAPTER 3

LEGENDS

Bob Griese played quarterback on the Dolphins' two championship teams. He was a smart, accurate passer. Griese often connected with Paul Warfield. Warfield was a speedy wide receiver. He made five straight Pro Bowls with Miami in the early 1970s.

Bob Griese made eight Pro Bowls during his career.

Miami's rushing attack was a three-man job. Fullback Larry Csonka hit the line of scrimmage like a bulldozer. Csonka teamed up with halfback Mercury Morris. In 1972, they both had at least 1,000 rushing yards. They were the first NFL teammates to do that in the same season. Jim Kiick changed the pace. He was a good receiver out of the backfield.

CLEARING THE WAY

Larry Csonka did his damage running up the middle. Miami's three best offensive linemen helped. Jim Langer played center. Larry Little played right guard. Both were future Hall of Famers. Bob Kuechenberg played left guard. He was a six-time Pro Bowl selection.

In the 1973 season,
Larry Csonka
was named Most
Valuable Player of
the Super Bowl.

23

Miami's defense was stacked with talent. Vern Den Herder recorded at least 10 sacks in three different seasons. Manny Fernandez was a run-stuffing defensive tackle. And Bill Stanfill racked up 18.5 sacks in 1973.

Other defenders stepped up in later years. Defensive end A. J. Duhe shined in 1977. He was named Defensive Rookie of the Year. And nose tackle Bob Baumhower was a five-time All-Pro pick.

Vern Den Herder makes a tackle during Miami's Super Bowl win over Washington.

Jake Scott made two interceptions during the Super Bowl. He ran one back 55 yards.

26

Nick Buoniconti joined the Dolphins in 1969. The linebacker was already a seven-year veteran. This experience made him the leader of the No-Name Defense.

Free safety Jake Scott was named to the Pro Bowl five times. He was the Most Valuable Player (MVP) of the Dolphins' first Super Bowl win. He intercepted two passes against Washington. Dick Anderson was another interception expert. He led the Dolphins in picks three times.

CHAPTER 4

RECENT HISTORY

In the 1983 draft, the Dolphins selected Dan Marino. He quickly became a star. In the 1984 season, Marino led the Dolphins back to the Super Bowl. But Miami lost to the San Francisco 49ers.

Dan Marino drops back to pass during the Super Bowl against San Francisco.

Mark Duper was a top wide receiver for Miami from 1982 to 1992.

The Dolphins made the playoffs eight times in the next 15 seasons. However, they didn't return to the Super Bowl. Marino ended his career after the 1999 season. After that, Miami made the playoffs two years in a row. But then the team hit a major skid.

PROTECTING THE LEGACY

In a 1985 game, the Chicago Bears visited Miami. At the time, the Bears were 12–0. But the Dolphins beat the Bears. This win protected the undefeated 1972 Dolphins' place in history.

Quarterback Chad Pennington led the Dolphins during their 2008 comeback season.

The Dolphins missed the playoffs the next six years. In 2007, they had their worst season ever. They went 1–15. But the Dolphins made history again in 2008. They went 11–5 and won their division. No team had done that one year after winning just one game.

WILDCAT STRIKE

The 2008 Dolphins changed football. They started using the Wildcat offense. On some plays, the center snapped the ball directly to a running back. The running back could then run or pass. The Wildcat sparked a trend across the league.

Miami's success was short-lived, though. The team missed the playoffs for years. But in 2020, the Dolphins selected quarterback Tua Tagovailoa in the draft. He was a scrambling lefty. In 2022 and 2023, he helped Miami make back-to-back playoffs.

MIAMI MIRACLE

In a 2018 game, Miami trailed the New England Patriots. It was 33–28. The Dolphins had the ball at their own 31-yard line. There was time for one more play. The quarterback passed. Then there were two laterals. Running back Kenyan Drake caught the second one. He outran the Patriots to the end zone. He scored a shocking, game-winning touchdown.

Tua Tagovailoa threw for 4,624 yards in 2023. That was the most in the NFL.

DAN MARINO

Quarterback Dan Marino joined the Dolphins in 1983. He soon shattered NFL passing records. In 1984, he threw for more than 5,000 yards. He was the first player to do so. He also tossed a record 48 touchdowns that season. The old record was 36.

Marino perfected the passing game. He threw bullet passes. And he mastered the quick release. This speed helped him avoid sacks.

Marino was the face of the Dolphins until 1999. During his career, he threw for more than 60,000 yards. At the time, that was an all-time NFL record.

DAN MARINO WAS THE NFL'S MVP OF THE 1984 SEASON.

CHAPTER 5

MODERN STARS

Dan Marino passed to plenty of great targets over the years. Mark Clayton caught 18 touchdown passes in 1984. That led the NFL. Clayton led the league again in 1988. Marino also threw to Mark Duper. Duper topped 1,000 receiving yards four times.

Mark Clayton had more than 1,300 receiving yards during the 1984 season.

Great offensive linemen blocked for Marino. They allowed few sacks throughout the 1980s. Center Dwight Stephenson was a big reason why. He burst off the snap to stop the rush. He was an All-Pro pick in five straight seasons. He became one of the best centers to play the game. Richmond Webb took over at left tackle in 1990. He protected Marino's blind side. Webb made seven straight Pro Bowls.

Dwight Stephenson blocks a Buffalo Bills pass rusher.

Zach Thomas was selected to the Pro Bowl seven times.

Opposing offenses feared defensive end Jason Taylor. He focused on sacking the quarterback. Linebacker Zach Thomas averaged nearly 10 tackles per game. Linebacker Cameron Wake joined Miami later. Like Taylor, he was a pass-rush specialist.

INTERCEPTION MACHINE

Sam Madison spent nine years leading the Miami secondary. He intercepted eight passes in 1998. The next year, he led the league with seven interceptions.

Tyreek Hill was one of the fastest players in the NFL. During a 2023 game, he ran 22 miles per hour (35 km/h).

In the early 2020s, the Dolphins turned the offense over to Tua Tagovailoa. He loved to throw the long ball. He often found wide receiver Tyreek Hill. Hill posted 1,799 receiving yards in 2023. That led the league.

Running back Raheem Mostert used his hard-charging style to rack up touchdowns. His 18 rushing touchdowns in 2023 topped the NFL.

JASON TAYLOR

Defensive end Jason Taylor spent 15 years in the NFL. Thirteen were with the Dolphins. He averaged 10 sacks per season.

Taylor peaked after Dan Marino left. The team's focus shifted to defense. Taylor's quickness helped him blow past offensive linemen. And his strength helped him take down quarterbacks. In 2002, Taylor led the NFL in sacks. Four years later, he was named the Defensive Player of the Year. That year, he posted 13.5 sacks. He also forced nine fumbles.

JASON TAYLOR RETURNED SIX FUMBLES FOR TOUCHDOWNS DURING HIS CAREER.

CHAPTER 6

TEAM TRIVIA

The Dolphins were the first major league sports team in Florida. They proved the state could support pro sports. Today, there are many major league teams in Florida. Miami is home to five of them.

The Miami area is home to more than six million people.

In 1971, Miami faced the Kansas City Chiefs in the playoffs. The game was tied after four quarters. Neither team scored in the first overtime. Nearly eight scoreless minutes passed in the second overtime. Finally, Miami kicked the game-winning field goal. It was the longest game in NFL history.

WINNING TRADITION

The Dolphins enjoyed an amazing 30-year run of success. Between 1970 and 1999, they had just two losing seasons. No other NFL team could make that claim.

Garo Yepremian (1) kicks a game-winning field goal during the 1971 playoffs.

Fans cheer during a Miami Dolphins game.

The Dolphins started using a new fight song in 1972. "Miami Dolphins Number One" was a big hit with fans. The team went undefeated that year. So, the Dolphins have stuck with the song ever since.

FALSE START

In 2009, the Dolphins recorded a new version of their fight song. They hired hip-hop artist T-Pain to do it. But fans didn't like it. The team quickly went back to the original song.

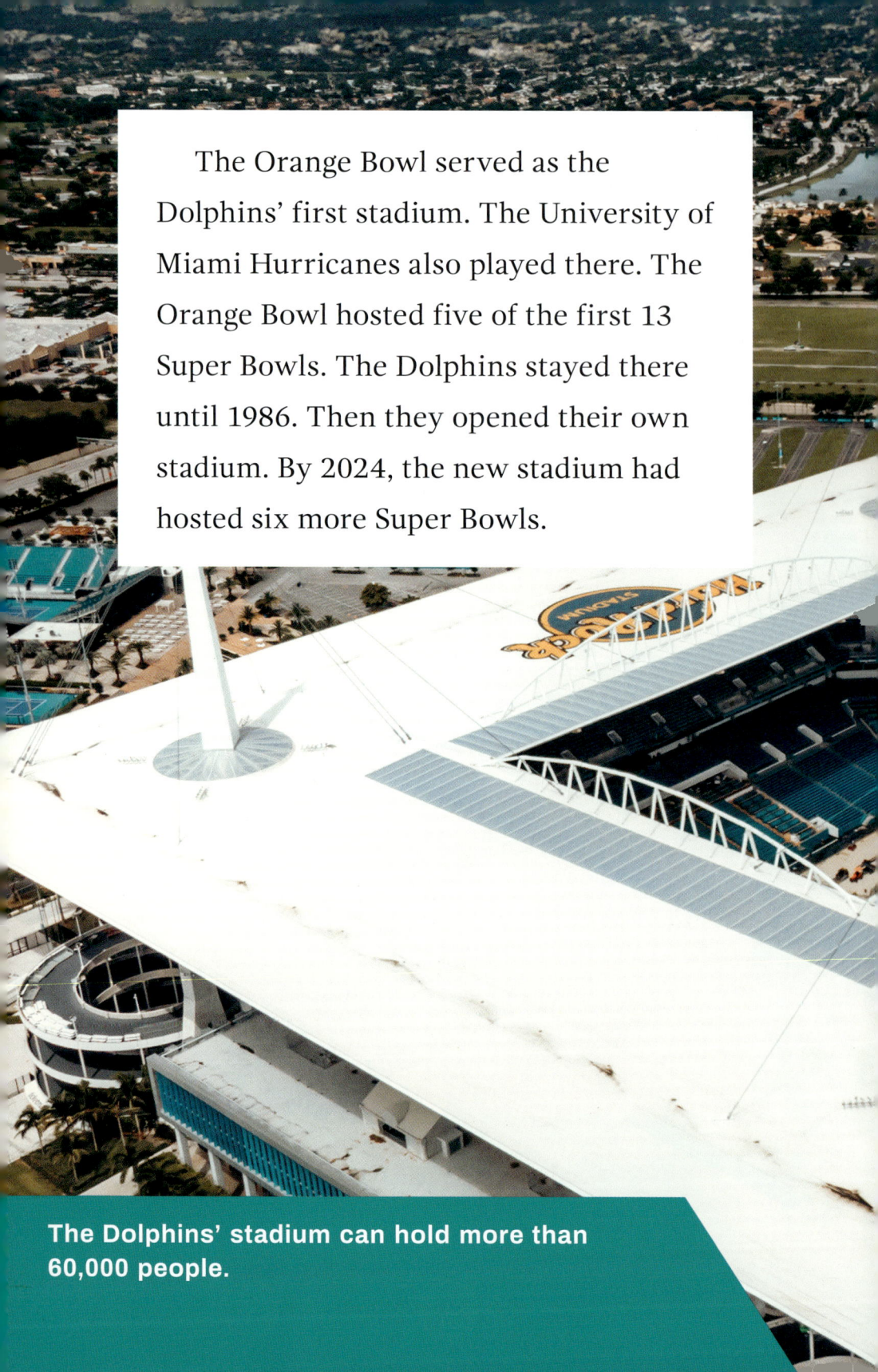

The Orange Bowl served as the Dolphins' first stadium. The University of Miami Hurricanes also played there. The Orange Bowl hosted five of the first 13 Super Bowls. The Dolphins stayed there until 1986. Then they opened their own stadium. By 2024, the new stadium had hosted six more Super Bowls.

The Dolphins' stadium can hold more than 60,000 people.

TEAM RECORDS

All-Time Passing Yards: 61,361
Dan Marino (1983–99)

All-Time Touchdown Passes: 420
Dan Marino (1983–99)

All-Time Rushing Yards: 6,737
Larry Csonka (1968–74, 1979)

All-Time Receiving Yards: 8,869
Mark Duper (1982–92)

All-Time Receiving Touchdowns: 81
Mark Clayton (1983–92)

All-Time Interceptions: 35
Jake Scott (1970–75)

All-Time Sacks: 131
Jason Taylor (1997–2007, 2009, 2011)

All-Time Scoring: 1,048
Olindo Mare (1997–2006)

All-Time Coaching Wins: 257
Don Shula (1970–95)

Super Bowl Titles: 2
(1972, 1973)

All statistics are accurate through 2023.

TIMELINE

1966 **1970** **1972** **1973** **1984**

The Miami Dolphins join the AFL as an expansion team.

The Dolphins become the first team to go undefeated and win the Super Bowl.

Dan Marino breaks the NFL records for most passing yards and most touchdown passes in a season.

The Dolphins become part of the NFL when it joins together with the AFL.

The Dolphins cruise to their second straight Super Bowl victory.

1995   **1997**   **2008**   **2018**   **2020**

The Dolphins draft defensive end Jason Taylor.

On December 9, the Dolphins shock the New England Patriots with a game-winning touchdown on the final play.

Don Shula retires after 26 years as the Dolphins' head coach.

One year after going 1–15, the Dolphins win their division with an 11–5 record.

The Dolphins draft quarterback Tua Tagovailoa with the No. 5 pick.

COMPREHENSION QUESTIONS

Write your answers on a separate piece of paper.

1. Write a paragraph that explains the main ideas of Chapter 2.

2. Who do you think was the greatest player in Dolphins history? Why?

3. Who led the No-Name Defense?
   A. Jason Taylor
   B. Dan Marino
   C. Nick Buoniconti

4. Why was the Dolphins' 2018 win over the New England Patriots so shocking?
   A. They won without scoring a touchdown.
   B. They hadn't won a game yet that season.
   C. They scored a long touchdown at the last moment.

5. What does **retired** mean in this book?

*Then they lost many stars. Some **retired**.*
Others moved on to different teams.

    A. changed positions

    B. ended their careers

    C. signed long contracts

6. What does **veteran** mean in this book?

The linebacker was already a seven-year
***veteran**. This experience made him the leader*
of the No-Name Defense.

    A. someone who cannot play a game

    B. someone who is new to the game

    C. someone who has played for a
        long time

Answer key on page 64.

GLOSSARY

division
In the NFL, a group of teams that make up part of a conference.

dynasty
A team that has a long period of success. The team usually wins several championships.

expansion team
A new team that is added to a league.

intercepted
Caught an opponent's pass as a defensive player.

laterals
Passes that go sideways or backward.

line of scrimmage
The place on the field where a play starts.

quick release
Taking a short amount of time to get the ball out of the quarterback's hands for a pass.

sacks
Plays that happen when a defender tackles the quarterback before he can throw the ball.

secondary
The defensive players, such as cornerbacks and safeties, who start the play farthest from the line of scrimmage.

specialist
A person who does one thing extremely well.

TO LEARN MORE

BOOKS

Gitlin, Marty. *The Greatest Quarterbacks of All Time*. San Diego: BrightPoint Press, 2021.

Goodman, Michael E. *Miami Dolphins*. Mankato, MN: Creative Education, 2023.

Olson, Ethan. *Great NFL Super Bowl Championships*. San Diego: BrightPoint Press, 2024.

ONLINE RESOURCES

Visit **www.apexeditions.com** to find links and resources related to this title.

ABOUT THE AUTHOR

Brendan Flynn is a San Francisco resident and an author of numerous children's books. In addition to writing about sports, Flynn also enjoys competing in triathlons, Scrabble tournaments, and chili cook-offs.

INDEX

ANSWER KEY:
1. Answers will vary; 2. Answers will vary; 3. C; 4. C; 5. B; 6. C